MW01172493

Honky Tonk Nights to Christian Lights

The Unforgettable Journey of a Music Promoter's Transformation

John A. Wilson, Jr.

2024 © John A. Wilson, Jr.

All rights reserved. Published 2024.

BIBLE SCRIPTURES

Scripture quotations marked (NLT) are taken from the Holy Bible, New Living Translation (NLT), Copyright © 1996, 2004, 2015 by Tyndale House Foundation. Used by permission of Tyndale House Publishers, a Division of Tyndale House Ministries, Carol Stream, Illinois 60188. All rights reserved.

Printed in the United States of America

www.lightthewayministry.com
5002 North 22nd Street Ozark, MO 65721
(417) 319-1338

Books › Christian Books & Bibles › Christian Living › Personal Memoirs

Paperback ISBN: 979-8-9909644-0-2
Hardback ISBN: 979-8-9909644-2-6
Audiobook ISBN: 979-8-9909644-3-3
eBook ISBN: 979-8-9909644-1-9
Library of Congress Control Number: 2024913296

INTRODUCTION

Today is the day I've been eagerly anticipating, and the excitement is electrifying. I'm sitting on a speaker—side stage—looking out on the largest crowd for any event I've ever organized. This moment is hitting me deeply. I'm filled with every imaginable emotion. I can't help but marvel at how someone like me, a small-town nobody, managed to bring together something of this magnitude! The dream I've carried since I first thought about becoming a concert promoter is becoming a reality right before my eyes in the form of this massive music festival! The dream, transformed into a vision through an encounter with Jesus, is now real! It's here!

I'm looking out on a huge sea of nearly 43,000 people, each one passionately singing along with the band. Their voices and movements call to mind undulating waves in the ocean, where each individual in the crowd contributes a distinct set of emotions, creating a dynamic and collective energy that transcends the usual musical experience. The energy is so intense, it feels as though a vibrant, spiritual force has enveloped the field, infusing everyone with an almost sacred vitality. It's not just about the music; it's about everyone present, sharing in this moment together. Tears flow freely as I absorb the overwhelming sense of awe, grappling with the profound realization that God has chosen to use me to bring about this experience. The journey leading up to this wasn't easy, that I have overcome - perhaps? that make this moment exceptionally special. The challenges, risks, and leaps of faith taken on my journey to this place and time were undeniably tough, but what I'm seeing before me is making every difficulty and every trial along the way feel absolutely worthwhile. Before this day would end, hundreds would embrace Jesus as their Lord and Savior, many would come to the baptismal waters, and many would attest to having experienced healing.

Thank you for picking up this book and coming along on this journey with me. In the pages that follow, you'll find highs and lows on the way to spiritual maturity and resilience. I hope my words will touch your heart and offer inspiration to your spirit. Shared stories have the power to connect us and remind us we are not alone in our struggles.

Before we jump into my story, I want to share some Bible passages with you. These set the stage for what is to come. Just as a seed grows into a plant that bears more seeds, every story of redemption reaches its full potential when shared with others. My story, and your story, are important and have the power to inspire and lift those with whom we share them. Do not let fear hold you back from sharing the transformative work God has done in your life. The enemy may try to silence you, but do not let him keep you from letting others know how God has turned your broken pieces into a beautiful masterpiece. Even though this book is short, it has taken me three years to get it down on paper. I had to learn to embrace the power of my story and to recognize the call I had to share it with you and the world.

In Psalm 66:16, we read: "Come and listen, all you who fear God, and I will tell you what he did for me" (NLT). And in Mark 5:19 is this: "Go home to your own people and tell them how much the Lord has done for you, and how he has had mercy on you" (NLT). And in 2 Corinthians 11:30: "If I must boast, I will boast of the things that show my weakness" (NLT).

Paul's example of sharing his story as a servant of Jesus in 2 Corinthians 11:23-33 serves as an inspiration for us to share our own testimonies with others. If you feel called to share your story but are unsure where to begin, start by reflecting on these three statements: "This is who I was. This is what Jesus did for me. This is who I am now." Ask God to reveal to you the person who needs to hear your story and be open to sharing your journey of faith with them. So, without further ado, allow me to share my redemption journey with you.

What can I say about John Wilson? I've known the man for thirty years, so when he and his wife, Beth, showed up to play softball, it was life as normal. What I wasn't ready for was what would happen over the following few weeks. It started with some choice words when he'd drop a pop fly, but it turned into a revival that has swept across the region. John has always been unapologetically John, so that meant, before Christ, he wasn't going to change who he was around Christians. Therefore, you never knew what John was going to say. People, though, just loved on him, and on Beth, his wife. John 13:35 says the world will recognize we are true followers of Jesus by the way we love others despite their actions. I would say, without a doubt, the way people loved John and Beth is what drew the two to a place of repentance.

John had been coming to Sunday night softball, an outreach of the church, for several weeks but, one Sunday morning, he showed up in worship. That turned into every Sunday morning, and that turned into his entire family coming to church. Over time, John came to the place where he knew he had to truly abandon his former life and surrender to Jesus. Shortly thereafter, Beth came to the altar to do the same. It was a place of genuine repentance; tears filled their eyes, and grace filled their hearts. It was glorious! In one conversation, John told me about concerts he put on, and I asked him: "Why not do a Christian show?" He hadn't given too much thought to that idea, but a bit later, he asked if we would host and help cover some of the cost if we brought in a Christian artist. BOOM! Seventh Day Slumber came to the little town of Stockton, Missouri. On the night of that first concert, 23 teens came to the altar to accept Christ as their Lord and were freed from struggles with suicide, freed from sin, given a forever hope. Miracles. John was a wreck and knew his life would never be the same. John abandoned his own will, picked up the cross, and began to carry it. Show after show, night after night, event after event, he was on a mission to "Make Jesus Famous." What was birthed was one of the greatest experiences in which I've had a part: Light The Way. I've watched John and Beth grow and mature over the years. We've had some great and hard conversations about ministry. I couldn't be more proud of the ministry John and Beth are leading and the way they love the world around them right where they are. They have indeed become beacons of light in a dark world.

John, I am beyond proud of you. Keep up the great work of loving your family, serving God, and making Jesus "famous" on earth.

Pastor Beau Norman
The Hill Church

AN APPRECIATION

There are people whom God brings into our lives for kingdom purposes. Such was true for John Wilson and me. Two people, each with different gifts and talents, whose destinies were knit together by God to combine music and Christian service in what is known today as Light the Way Ministry. It was the spring of 2017 when God put John in my path. He was a brand new, born-again believer. He came to my church seeking volunteers and donors to help him with a plan to produce a Christian music festival in his hometown. The suggestion came from his Pastor, Beau Norman, the man who had led him to Jesus. Pastor Beau would soon become my pastor also, as God began weaving our three hearts together for kingdom ministry. It seems we can't tell our individual life stories without including one another and the impact that we've had on each other's lives for the purposes of God.

On our first encounter, I introduced myself to him and asked: "Who is leading your Prayer Tent? I'm a prayer warrior, I love to pray for people, and I'd love to be a part of your Prayer Team!" He stared at me with a puzzled look on his face and replied: "Lady, I have no idea what a Prayer Tent is. I don't even know what you're talking about, I'm just trying to put on a music festival." I said: "But, you need to have a Prayer Tent, so we can pray for people! Pick me to lead the Prayer Tent, and I'll bring a team of prayer warriors, Bibles, tracts, and everything else we need for people to get saved, healed, delivered, and set free in Jesus' name!"

I met him at his office the next week. We talked; he shared his vision. God spoke to my heart that day, impressing upon me that He had put us together so my husband Stanley and I could become John's spiritual mother and father, called to mentor him on his faith walk, called to be his spiritual covering over the ministry. In the years that followed, we watched God grow Light the Way, but more importantly, my husband

and I watched John grow in his faith and his relationship with the Lord. Soon his wife, Beth, and their children followed in his footsteps as they too gave their hearts and lives to Jesus. We were there to be a part of them getting baptized as well. Paul said in 3 John 1:4, "I could have no greater joy than to hear that my children are following the truth." (NLT). That's exactly how I feel about our John Boy. (The nickname my husband and I affectionately call John.)

Over the nearly 60 events on which John and I have worked together throughout my seven years with the ministry, I've been a witness to John's drive and determination to push the ministry to the next level, always wanting to grow and get better with everything he does for Light the Way.

From where we began—with a few dollars in our bank account and a tiny shoebox of an office with crooked walls and uneven floors that had us propping books under our desks and chairs just to do our work—to seeing thousands of people give their hearts to Jesus, it's all been a miraculous work of God. To God be the Glory!

John has overcome a lot in his life to get where he is today. I know his story firsthand; I've watched it unfold before my eyes; I've seen the transformation God has made in him. As his Spiritual Mama, I couldn't be more proud of him for the work he has done and continues to do for the Lord.

John Boy, what did Mama always tell you to do? "WRITE IT DOWN!" And now you have. Congratulations on writing your book! Good job, son, you get a cookie!

Love you, Mama Donna

Donna Lind: Light the Way Ministry Board President, Assistant Festival Director and Prayer Team Director; Founder of Healing Hope Ministry; Prayer & Care Pastor for The Hill Church Bolivar; Author; Speaker; Christian Counselor; retired Light the Way Ministry Pastor, Secretary and Treasurer; and Mama to John Boy. www.donnalind.com

TABLE OF CONTENTS

Introduction   3

Foreword   5

An Appreciation   7

Chapter 1: The Journey Begins   10

Chapter 2: Longing and Belonging   17

Chapter 3: Bartending and a Concert   25

Chapter 4: My First Gig!   31

Chapter 5: Going Against My Better Judgment!   37

Chapter 6: A Voice I Think I'd Heard Before   43

Chapter 7: The Dream   48

Chapter 8: It was the Field!!   53

Chapter 9: Getting Out of the Way   59

Chapter 10: A Promise Made to God   63

Conclusion   68

1

THE
JOURNEY
BEGINS

My journey began in the place I called home: Stockton, Missouri. In that small town, I got myself entangled in a web of trouble with the local authorities, making choices that—in hindsight—I now see as unwise. I was indulging in drugs and alcohol and evidencing a rebellious streak that defined the early chapters of my life.

My childhood and youth, from ages seven to seventeen, were far from ideal. Raised in a poor home, I knew little in the way of material wealth or comfort. My household consisted of my stepmother, my half-sister, my step-sister, and my biological father. Dad, a truck driver, was rarely at home. Sometimes, I would accompany him on the open road, and over the years, I often found myself daydreaming about the future, harboring the belief that one day I would become a truck driver like my father.

Isolated and hungry for a different life, my only entertainment was a trusty radio that played music, music that provided a comforting escape from the starkness of my circumstances. Music possessed a unique and remarkable ability to provide me with comfort and solace, effectively easing my feelings of loneliness. It was as if the music had an innate power to connect with my emotions, offering a sense of companionship and understanding during times when I felt most isolated. I spent countless hours immersed in the world of radio, listening especially to Delilah on iHeart. I can still hear her soothing voice in my head coming alongside the perfectly-timed songs that brought me comfort.

When I think back to my teenage years, one particular picture stands out in my mind: the view from my basement window. You see, my room was in the lower level, a cave-like, dark, dank place, with an almost oppressive chill that instilled the feeling of being in a desolate place. I couldn't help but feel a pang of longing whenever I glanced outside. Through that one small window in that space, I would catch glimpses of the neighbor kids with, what seemed to be, carefree spirits and playful energy. Oh, how I yearned to be out there with them, escaping the confines of my basement hole, joining them in their adventures. But my strict stepmother wouldn't let me go out, and my father was often away on the road, so he wasn't around much to intervene. In those years, my only hours outside were spent at school or at church.

From ages 12 to 17, I was involved with a congregation, the Stockton Assembly of God Church. I played drums with the worship team and joined the youth group. My participation came about largely due to the influence of the worship leader, Scott. Scott quickly became a father-like figure to me as I was growing up. He saw the dysfunction in my house and the restrictions that prevented me from doing many of the normal things a teenager would typically be able to do. Scott took me to church and other places, and often communicated with my father and stepmother. He made it appear he agreed with the punishments my parents would impose so they would be more inclined to let me work with him. He owned a carpet store 20 miles away from my house, and it was through him that I learned about business. Scott also taught me how to drive, how to do math, how to budget, and—since he owned a carpet store—how to lay carpet. He was married (his wife, Cindy, was also on the worship team), and they had two kids, one a son the same age as me. With Scott's encouragement, I ended up joining the worship team. I received my very first Bible, a high school graduation gift, from Randall Hayward, pastor of this church.

Stepping back a year, I should note that I didn't get the gift of a bike till I was 16. I can still feel the excitement that was mine as it was presented to me. It was a milestone marker signaling newfound independence, freedom. But my joy was short-lived, as I found myself grounded, sent to my room on that very same day. It felt like an agonizing tease, knowing my new bike was waiting just outside but also knowing I was being denied the thrill of riding it.

Those moments when I finally had the chance to take my bike for a spin, up and down our very short driveway, were pure exhilaration. It was a small space, but to me, it felt like the open road, a canvas for my budding sense of adventure. With each wobbly start and determined push of the pedals, I felt a surge of self-determination propelling me forward. Learning how to ride that bike became about more than just developing a skill; it was a testament to my perseverance and resilience and the development within me of a strong work ethic.

Despite the difficulties I faced, I emerged with a resilience and determination that instilled in me fearlessness when it came to hard work. At the age of 17, when I was in my junior year of high school, the misery in my home became too much, and I decided to strike out on my own. With a heavy heart, I gathered up all my belongings and hastily packed them into two trash bags. At that moment, I made the courageous choice to leave behind the only home I had ever known, leaving behind the past, leaving behind that dark basement room, and embracing an uncertain future. From that point forward, I vowed never to look back, embarking on a journey of self-discovery and forging my own path.

The weight of responsibility pressed heavily upon my shoulders, and I was compelled to secure a full-time job just to make ends meet. I managed to persevere and even earned my high school diploma. Even so, I couldn't escape the shadow of my upbringing. I could say that drugs and alcohol defined my life, but in reality, it was the constant search for a sense of belonging that truly consumed me. For as long as I can remember, I've always had an intense desire to be the main focus of attention. It felt like my very existence relied on being the center of everyone's gaze, and I would do whatever it took to achieve that recognition. I was unwavering in my relentless pursuit of the spotlight. In fact, during my junior and senior years of high school, I had the unique experience of living on my own and renting my own house. My place quickly became known as the go-to party destination for my peers. I recall a time when I threw a bash that ended up attracting the attention of the police and resulted in a frightening encounter where a gun was pointed. Yes, it was one of the largest parties I had ever thrown. There were nearly a hundred people in attendance, most of whom I wouldn't even consider close friends. They were primarily drawn to the event for the availability of alcohol. This party stretched into the early morning hours before I decided it was time to bring it to a close. Unfortunately, not everyone agreed with that idea. Barely an hour after my attempt to shut things

Honky Tonk Nights to Christian Lights by John A. Wilson, Jr.

13

down, there was an audacious break-in attempt at my house. The target? A keg of beer that I had securely chained to the pipes of my bathtub. The intruders forcefully entered through a window, completely ripping out the air conditioner unit.

In a state of panic, I dialed 911, and soon enough, the police arrived with guns drawn, pointing towards a bush where one of my supposed "friends" was hiding. As I reflect on the events of that night, I realize my own intoxication clouded my judgment. I chose not to pursue legal action against those involved. The night eventually came to a close, leaving me with a mixture of fear and a valuable lesson learned. It became evident that not everyone who attended the party was a true friend but rather individuals who were solely interested in exploiting the availability of free drinks. Looking back, I can see that my relentless pursuit of attention, and my choice to host extravagant parties, was driven by a deep desire to fit in and find a sense of belonging. I believed that, by being the center of attention, I would finally feel accepted and valued by those around me. However, what happened at that particular party served to impress upon me that true friendship and genuine connections cannot be built solely on superficial motives or the pursuit of popularity. It was a valuable lesson that taught me the importance of surrounding myself with people who genuinely care about me rather than seeking validation through attention-seeking behaviors. As a consequence of what occurred at that party, the landlord evicted me.

I was now homeless and needed a new place to live. Even in my present situation, the idea of returning to my parent's home was unimaginable, completely out of the question. The idea of being trapped in that dark, gloomy basement room and not having freedom was something I was not willing to consider. So, I started looking for a real friend who might let me stay at his or her place until I could get back on track. Fortunately, I had a friend named Jared who came to my rescue. Jared was still living with his parents, but his home was welcoming and supportive. At last, I found a place where I could experience a sense of stability.

Despite there being more good days than bad, I couldn't shake the feeling of being a third wheel in my friend's home with his family. It wasn't their fault; they never made me feel left out or unwanted. It was just a lingering sense of not quite belonging, a constant reminder that I was different. I watched as his parents shared inside jokes and laughed together; their bond seemingly unbreakable. They had known each other for years, building a life together long before I came along. I was the newcomer, the addition to their already-established household.

This family had a connection I wasn't really used to seeing. They shared secrets, confided in each other, and had a camaraderie that I longed to share. They always did things together, experiencing the ups and downs of life side by side. I, on the other hand, always felt like the odd one out. I was the troubled one. I was the black sheep. It wasn't that they intentionally excluded me; they tried their best to include me in their activities and conversations. But I always felt like I was on the outside looking in. I couldn't fully relate to their memories or understand their shared experiences. I was a piece trying to fit into a puzzle that was already complete.

I often found myself retreating into my own world, seeking solace in my own company. I immersed myself in late-night parties, music, and hobbies that allowed me to escape the feeling of being the odd one out. Over time, I learned to accept that being a third wheel didn't make me any less loved or valued. It was simply a part of my unique journey within this family. I realized my role was different, and that was okay. I had my own strengths and my own perspectives to offer.

While the feeling of being a third wheel never completely disappeared, it became less of a concern for me. I learned to cherish the moments of connection and love that we shared rather than the moments I felt apart. I realized family isn't just about blood ties or commonly-held histories; it's about the love and support given to each other, despite of differences.

So, even though I still felt like an outsider at times, I knew—deep down—that I was an integral part of my "adopted" family. I may have been different, but I was loved unconditionally, faults and all. And that was enough to make me feel like I belonged.

Nevertheless, I was a nuisance for Jared and his family. I would come and go as I pleased, partying to the extreme and occasionally bringing guests to Jared's house, which undoubtedly raised issues for his family. I came to realize it was time for me to make a change and to stop causing pain. I remain grateful for the lessons I learned while with them: the value of working diligently and responsibly; the value found in loving one another.

2

LONGING AND BELONGING

Once again, my deep yearning for a sense of belonging and acceptance drove me to embark on a search for the next opportunity or experience that would fulfill those desires. I was constantly on the lookout for new avenues and connections, hoping to find a place where I could truly feel involved. When I was 18 and approaching the end of my time at Jared's house, I decided to join the local volunteer fire department and first responders team. Jared served with me for a season.

This choice allowed me to channel my desire for involvement and acceptance into a meaningful and impactful endeavor. By becoming a part of this dedicated group of individuals, I found a sense of purpose and belonging within a community that valued service and helping others. It was a transformative experience that allowed me to contribute to the well-being of my community while also finding a sense of camaraderie and acceptance with my fellow volunteers.

While the experiences and connections I made through this service brought some fulfillment, I was still grappling with the same old underlying issues of loneliness, fear of rejection, feelings of inadequacy, feeling "less," needing to be wanted, needing to be valued, needing to make a difference. Despite my best efforts, I would consistently find myself gravitating towards the familiar setting of the local bar or weekend parties, desperately attempting to blend in, to find my place in the crowd. My go-to drugs were weed, Bud Light, Jager Bombs, and different kinds of shots. I wanted to be the life of every party; I was always desperate to be accepted. I suppose I was looking for a "substitute" family to fill the vacuum inside.

On weekends, I would hop from one gathering to another, trying hard to fit in and, at the same time, stand out. On other days, I would switch gears and become a firefighter, facing dangerous situations to save lives and protect property. There was a big difference between the fun and socializing of the weekends and the serious and selfless work of service. I had to balance these two different parts of my life, seeking acceptance while also doing my duty to help others. It was a tough but rewarding experience that showed me the different sides of who I am.

Even after almost a decade of living this double life, the lingering question persisted: how could I overcome the constant yearning for acceptance?

When I was 17, I learned—by reading my birth certificate—that the woman I thought was my biological mother was, instead, my stepmother. Through family conversations, I got my biological mother's name: Christine. I was told I was born with pneumonia and other health issues, and was extremely small due to the lack of proper nutrition while in the womb. My real mom was just 16 when she had me, just 15 when she had my sister, and she didn't want anything to do with either of us. I was told I was on my deathbed as an infant, and my mom left the hospital, leaving me in the care of my grandmother (who has since passed).

I didn't have much of a relationship with my biological mother growing up because my stepmom and dad wouldn't let me see her. Maybe that was because they didn't want me to find out the truth about things? Well, when I graduated from high school, I became more curious and wondered if she would want me in her life. Via Google searches, I discovered she was living in a community south of Kansas City and was working in a bar. I arranged to meet her. A group of church friends and I mustered the courage to take a road trip to Kansas City. As we drove to the bar where we were to meet, I was filled with trepidation, but I also had a glimmer of hope within me that this encounter might provide answers and perhaps even some confirmation of being wanted and valued. I met her but spent a very short time with her. It was embarrassing, and I wanted to go home. I found no acceptance with her. I came away feeling deeply hurt and incredibly confused. The encounter, instead of providing the closure and connection I had longed for, only served to complicate matters and left me grappling with more unanswered questions. It was a difficult and painful experience, one that left me questioning my identity and my place in the world.

Overwhelmed by the pain and confusion that consumed me, I made the impulsive decision to run—to run away from everything and everybody. I fled from my church, my town, everything that was familiar. It was a desperate attempt to escape the turmoil within me, to find solace and clarity in a new and unknown environment. In the moment, I believed distance and change would bring me the peace and understanding I so desperately craved.

In my quest for a fresh start and a deeper sense of belonging, I discovered I had a stepbrother who happened to live in Saint Joseph, Missouri, my place of birth. This newfound connection presented an opportunity for me to forge a bond with someone who shared a familial tie, someone with whom I might find kinship and understanding even in unfamiliar territory. Intrigued by the prospect of building a relationship with him and seeking to be new in a different environment, I made the decision to head towards this northern part of Missouri, leaving behind my past, eager to open a new chapter in my life.

For a short season, I worked a good job with a healthy salary in that city. Since nobody knew me there, it was a chance for a fresh start. To my surprise, I discovered my stepbrother was quite the party enthusiast himself! While I was living with him, I was introduced to the world of gambling, engaging in high-stakes games with individuals I should not have associated with. I played cards, risking every last dollar I had. I experienced wins and losses, but it wasn't too long before I realized I was developing yet another addiction, an addiction-not only to gambling but to the company of people in a different social circle. To my surprise, I learned my stepbrother was involved in a biker gang, and I could sense myself being pulled into that world.

No more church life for me. I fully immersed myself in this new edgier life. This "family" I had found provided me with a sense of protection and security. I felt ten-feet tall and bulletproof. My new brothers connected me to one woman after another, but I was still into the same old drugs and alcohol. Before I knew it, I found myself caught up in a lifestyle where partying every night had become the norm. Engaging in fights every night became a regular part of my routine, fueling an attitude that made me feel invincible and unstoppable in pursuing whatever or whomever I desired. Countless times, my stepbrother and I launched into heated fights over girls, despite the fact that he was married.

Night after night in bars, seeking affection, gambling, and running with biker buddies started to wear on me. Many nights, I'd lie in bed with one eye open, on edge, fearing I might be hunted down by someone seeking revenge for my involvement with his woman or coming to collect some gambling debt I had accumulated.

Feeling the weight of my sorry choices and the dangerous path on which I was traveling, I realized I needed to go back home. After about a year, marked by two new tattoos and the nickname "Fish," I made the decision to leave Saint Joseph for good, never to return. I relocated to Springfield, Missouri, and quickly secured a stable position with the well-known telephone company, MCI. I established connections with devout individuals from a local congregation known as Cornerstone. I quickly became deeply immersed in the life of the church again, dedicating my time to serving whenever its doors were open. I believed I had finally found my purpose or, at least, that's what I thought at the time. While I was with the congregation, the church introduced a program called Master's Commission, an intensive four-year discipleship program that bore similarities to a Christian-oriented boot camp. In this program, we were prohibited from holding outside employment, and we lived on the church campus itself.

During this period, I met a girl who appeared to have her life in perfect order. I pursued a relationship with her based on my desire for acceptance. She seemed to have her spiritual life well-organized, and in my bid to get her attention, I enrolled in the Master's Commission program. I sidestepped the program's strict no-dating-for-the-initial-two-years rule and secretly visited her. I did my best to conceal this breach from the leaders as much as I could. Though the program was intended to instill discipline, discipleship, and leadership, I couldn't help but see it as more of a Christian slavery program. We were always working around the church or at Christian events. One event was different from anything else in which the church participated. Prepping for this took weeks and weeks! I can remember the security needed to be top-notch for a guest speaker who was coming in. This event was so large it couldn't be held at the church but instead was held at the John Q. Hammons Arena (later renamed the Great Southern Bank Arena). So, I can remember working tirelessly at the arena all day. The only thing I knew about this event was that a very spiritual man would introduce an odd method of interacting with God.

When the event began, I was seated with my fellow students in the nosebleed section of the venue, observing the spectacle. I can vividly recall my reluctance to be there and my disbelief at what I was witnessing. People appeared to be falling all over the place as if they were stumbling over one another. It seemed like people had no control over themselves. Worship music was pouring out from the stage, and as I looked around, the only thought in my head was about asking God, "Is this real?" I closed my eyes and simply uttered, "God, if you're real, prove it to me!" I opened my eyes, and to my astonishment, I was suddenly on the main stage. I had no idea how I had moved from the nosebleed section to this prominent spot. I stood at the side of the stage, watching people approaching the preacher. He would say things to them, and they would either fall down or lose control of their bodies. I was next!

A man in all white approached me while I was being guided closer to him by several very large and tall men in suits who were behind me. When he came within about ten feet of me, I looked at him in sheer astonishment. Then, he paused and uttered these words, "YOU, YOUNG MAN, WILL LEAD THOUSANDS UPON THOUSANDS, UPON THOUSANDS TO THE KINGDOM OF GOD! NOW GO IN THE PEACE OF GOD!" For some reason, I just felt extremely weak. I don't recall falling down, but I did feel some kind of power, like 'I can take on the world' kind of power. I remember trying to make my way back to my seat, but I kept stumbling and bumping into people. As I did, those individuals would fall and start shaking as if they were experiencing seizures. It got to the point when the men in suits had to come get me and pull me away. It was an experience I had never felt before, nor have I experienced it since.

Fast forward, I was left utterly speechless and unable to provide any explanation for what had transpired. Consequently, I simply brushed it off with excuses. One of those excuses was the fact I was still pursuing the girl I'd been going against the program's leadership to visit. That breach of the rules would ultimately result in me getting kicked out of the program.

Now, I was in a situation where I had no job, no place to call home, and I was back to facing a familiar set of challenges. At this point, I had reached 20 years of age, on the cusp of turning 21. Consequently, I found myself staying wherever I could, returning to the bar scene, but this time, it felt like a different ballgame. Springfield's nightlife gravitated towards nightclubs. Night in and night out, I found myself drawn back into the bar scene, but still with no direction.

I then made the choice to embark on a significant career shift. Revisiting my childhood aspirations, I thought to myself, "I'm going to enroll in trucking school to pursue a career as an over-the-road truck driver." I understand what you might be thinking: "What on earth is going on with this person?" At every turn, it seemed like I would run into some form of trouble. But this time, I was convinced that enrolling in trucking school and pursuing a career as a truck driver would finally bring the solution to all my life's challenges. So, I boarded the next Greyhound bus to Salt Lake City, Utah, where the trucking school I wanted to attend was located. Upon arrival in the city, I distinctly recall feeling like this was exactly where I was meant to be! Nothing in this place was going to divert my attention from this new path I had chosen. The first day of school began with what appeared to be an interview process as a preliminary step before full acceptance into the school. I can vividly recall the instructor addressing us in a large group setting, emphasizing that these interviews would be rigorous. The goal was to bring any hidden issues or secrets to light, leaving no skeletons in the closet. The instructors were

CHAPTER 2

thorough in their inquiries, and they created an atmosphere where it seemed as if they had the ability to uncover any falsehood.

The interrogation was so intense that, as I started my interview, I had the sense my entire history was under scrutiny. Surprisingly, this was one of the few periods in my young adulthood when I had minimal involvement with drugs. I genuinely had nothing to conceal or fabricate. However, the instructor appeared to have a different perspective. He must have detected the stress and nervousness in my demeanor. With every response I provided, he straightforwardly accused me of lying. About ten minutes into the interview, the instructor abruptly dismissed me, announcing I would not be admitted to the school, I needed to pack my belongings, and I needed to leave immediately. I was completely shocked by this sudden turn of events. I remember feeling lost at the time, and my fear of not feeling accepted immediately swept over me. In addition, I was now forced to find my own way home, but where was "home" now? I had no money, and I wasn't about to take another five-day trip on a Greyhound bus. Where could I go? During my brief visit to the school, a friend, who was just as shocked as I was by the news, generously offered to pay for my plane ticket so I could return home—to Stockton.

The idea of flying was incredibly daunting for me. It was to be my first time in an airport, my first time in the air, and I had no clue about my next destination or how to get where I was going. The only option I had was Stockton. I checked in at the desk. My nerves were on high alert. Not knowing what to expect, I realized, at that moment, I had a fear of flying. The fact I was all by myself was not helping. When I reached the gate, I was shocked to discover my flight was delayed by a staggering 28 hours. With no funds, nowhere to turn, and stranded in— what appeared to me to be—the largest and most intimidating airport, I felt utterly helpless. At this moment, I was literally feeling like Tom Hanks in the movie "Terminal."

24

3

BARTENDING AND A CONCERT

Honky Tonk Nights to Christian Lights by John A. Wilson, Jr.

25

Finally, back home! A series of events led me back into familiar routines. I found myself in the bar scene every weekend while also volunteering in firefighting and first responding. Fortunately, I secured a place to live independently and landed a job tending bar at the watering hole I frequented. People there were my family, or seemed as much. As a result, I made connections with several weekenders and regulars. I recall an elderly lady who often stopped in; she didn't drink, but she came by every weekend to watch karaoke. She was known as Grandma Shirley! She was everyone's favorite! She enjoyed watching me sing, and danced enthusiastically at the bar. I admit I did some foolish things, all in an attempt to attract attention.

Grandma Shirley was one with whom I could be real and joke with. She had consistently advised me to find a girlfriend. I spent the majority of my days in the bar, working, drinking, and living the life of the party guy. Forgetting all my past church experiences, I worked toward gaining the acceptance of my bar family. The people at the church had never made me feel welcome; they seemed to me to be a group of judgmental individuals. To be honest, very few of the relationships I had with church people appeared to be genuine. I tried to persuade some to join me at the bar, and I did succeed a few times. It's not a proud moment in my life, but I want this book to be candid, so there it is.

The weekend had arrived, and here came Grandma Shirley! I always looked forward to her arrival at the bar because it meant the night was going to be enjoyable and full of fun. However, on this particular night, she walked in with a clear objective in mind. She'd seen me go through one relationship after another, each one ending in heartbreak. There was so much sorrow in nearly every one of those. In each connection I found myself in and out of, it seemed the girl I was with would later turn out to be involved with other people as well.

Grandma Shirley was well aware of my relationship troubles. So, she approached me and said, "I have someone I want you to meet." She told me this girl was sweet and worked as a bartender at a different watering hole in the neighboring town. She didn't have much more information to share about this girl, but—given my vulnerable state—I didn't need much more. I was all in! After a few weeks had gone by, I managed to secure a weekend off, and I headed over to the neighboring town to meet the girl Grandma Shirley was so eager for me to meet. It just so happened this town was hosting a festival, an outdoor picnic, which was akin to a small-town carnival. I can remember at one point being mesmerized by the outdoor concert and music on this picnic's main stage.

It was most likely my first time being at a concert, if you would even call it that. People, lots in lawn chairs, and some old-school street square dancing. As I walked into the local bar, where I was supposed to meet Grandma Shirley, my eyes were immediately drawn to a woman sitting on the other side of the bar. We couldn't help but steal glances at each other, silently admiring one another's looks. Finally, Grandma Shirley and her son made the connection between the two of us, recognizing the attraction that had already been brewing between us. I guess it is safe to say we were strongly attracted to each other. We quickly hit it off and found a deep connection. Feeling a strong desire to spend more time together, I extended an invitation for Bethany to join me at my bar. Arranged through a series of calls over the next few weeks, we set a time for her to come to my bar; but she didn't come alone. She brought two of her girlfriends with her. We closed the bar down that night.

Finally, I found a companion with whom I felt secure and comfortable. We grew closer, and our relationship deepened as the months flew by. Six months on, we discovered we were expecting our first daughter. The news brought a mix of excitement and uncertainty, but we were determined to navigate this new chapter of our lives together. Recognizing that bartending wouldn't provide the stability we needed, we made the decision to move from Stockton to Springfield, Missouri, in search of better career opportunities. It was there that I landed a job as a new car salesman at a local Kia dealership, hoping this career path would provide the support we were seeking for our family. I found the work rewarding and I was earning a substantial income for the first time. That brought a sense of accomplishment and financial stability. As I honed my skills and gained experience, I quickly rose through the ranks, eventually becoming one of Kia's top salesmen in the region. It was a testament to my hard work, dedication, and ability to connect with customers, and it filled me with a sense of pride and achievement.

Fast-forwarding about a year, Beth and I welcomed our first daughter into the world. Even with the responsibility and joy of parenthood upon us, we were reluctant to let go of our past habits. Beth and I continued our daily routine of drinking and smoking. For Beth, getting high was a daily ritual, while I found myself gradually distancing from smoking weed, although alcohol remained a constant. We walked a delicate balance between our desire to retain aspects of our former selves and our need to adapt to and prioritize our roles as parents. The economy experienced a serious downturn, and the car industry was struggling. I couldn't fully support my family as I had hoped. Consequently, we decided to take the necessary step of moving back to Stockton.

Around this time, I managed to secure a new job at a magazine delivery company. This opportunity held great potential for growth and offered promising advancements. Not only did I have access to a company vehicle, but I also had the freedom to set my own hours. Moreover, I didn't have the constant pressure of a boss scrutinizing my every move on a daily basis. This job provided me with ample windshield time. I would turn up the radio and simply drive, allowing my mind to wander. Surprisingly, I did some of my best thinking at the wheel. However, there was still a battle raging on the home front. Despite our move to Stockton and the addition of a second child to our family, we were unable to overcome our addictions.

Beth and I waged our own internal battles. Beth found herself grappling with alcohol and marijuana while I wrestled with pornography and alcohol consumption. Despite my wife's efforts, I couldn't shake the feeling that my desires were not being fulfilled. Given our history, we both felt trapped in a cycle that seemed familiar and comfortable. Consequently, we found ourselves returning to our not-so-great old habits. I distinctly recall numerous occasions, even on a nightly basis, when Beth would get high, or we would spend our weekends closing down the bar. We found ourselves living a paycheck-to-paycheck existence. Beth worked part-time at the local Sonic, while I discovered my job—that had initially appeared to be so promising—was a dead-end. I was becoming complacent.

Bright spots for me were found on the road, blaring the radio, letting the music wash over me, igniting my imagination. Each song became a soundtrack to my daydreams, fueling visions of what it would be like to attend the concerts I heard about in the advertisements. Thoughts of seeing my favorite artists perform live filled me with excitement and longing, transforming the monotony of the road into journeys of dreams and aspirations.

The one thing that consistently lifted my spirits was music. Beth and I shared a deep love for music. A talented singer, Beth would often be found singing. Every weekend, we would make it a point to go to the bar for karaoke sessions. These moments provided a temporary escape from our home struggles and allowed us to immerse ourselves in the carefree joy of our shared love for music. Unfortunately, our financial struggles often led to heated arguments. There were all too many times when we found ourselves unable to pay bills or buy groceries because we had spent our money on drugs or alcohol. To make matters worse, Beth would sometimes go behind my back and take out small payday loans, usually around $200 or $300, to fuel our addictions or get us through the weekend. We endured a prolonged season of relying on payday loans, dealing with bad credit, and constantly facing financial hardship with little to no money.

Beth sought her escape through drugs or alcohol, while I found solace in my return to music. I would think of the times in childhood when I would be confined to my room, feeling alone and afraid, when the little radio served as my lifeline. Playing music brought me comfort and transported me to a different world. One particularly memorable moment in our marriage was when Beth and I attended our first major outdoor country music festival. I would often hear about this event on the radio on my driving routes, and it would fill me with excitement. I longed to attend, but deep down, I knew we couldn't afford it. Then, one day, a stroke of luck came across the airwaves. There was an announcement on the radio about volunteers needed to help hand out flyers at the event. In the way of compensation, they were offering free tickets. I could hardly contain my excitement. This was the opportunity I had been waiting for—a chance to experience a live concert firsthand! I wasted no time in getting us signed up for the opportunity. We were thrilled at the prospect of seeing Tim McGraw and OneRepublic perform live. It was a dream come true for me.

The day came, and we arrived at a big field with a huge stage and lots of equipment. I was amazed by everything I saw! We went to the tent to check in for volunteering, but of course, we were more interested in the concert. We took the papers we were supposed to give out, but we only did it for a few minutes before throwing the rest away. Then, we went as close to the stage as we could. As I stood there, taking in the sights and sounds of the event, I found myself captivated by the behind-the-scenes logistics and operations. The stage setup, the crew working tirelessly, and the overall organization of the event fascinated me more than the actual songs performed or any specific on-stage moments. I can't recall much about the performances as my attention was drawn to the intricate workings behind the scenes. It was then I realized I wanted to be involved in that type of work. I had no clue how or where to start, but I knew this was something I wanted! I knew, without a doubt, that I would figure out how to get into the music business. Nothing was going to stop me.

Continuing to grapple with our addictions and other daily challenges, it appeared as though I wouldn't be able to break free from the struggle. Beth expressed it best: in this phase of our lives, it just felt like we met each other's representatives. It seemed as though I wasn't able to move the needle of getting into the music industry.

4

MY FIRST GIG!

A moment arrived when I bumped into a local artist, a member of a country music band. Country music resonated with me, and I was certain it was the genre I should pursue. I distinctly recall watching the CMT awards show on TV, lost in daydreams of a future where I would be there myself one day. So, I did a bunch of research to figure out how to make contacts with artists, how to book gigs; I basically learned everything I could so I could work with the local artist. I created my first music Industry company, called "Highway Promotion, LLC." It wasn't long before I had my first artist signing with J.R. Woods. I created my own agreements. I was well on my way! Beth and I made the decision together that we would figure out how to be a family at the same time. As I was launching Highway Promotions, LLC, my very first music industry company, I was also working full-time as a magazine delivery driver. This was no small feat, but I was determined to make it work. All the while, Beth and I were in the middle of purchasing our first home, adding another layer of excitement and responsibility to our lives. It was a whirlwind of activity and challenges, but I was driven by a passion for music and a vision for the future. Then, we—somehow— succeeded in purchasing our first home, gaining a First Time Home Buyers Credit in the process!

While I was passionately pursuing my dreams, Beth had her own aspirations. With a deep love for movies of all genres, she immersed herself in cinema, eagerly consuming films and sharing her perspectives with our friends. It didn't take long for us to realize that in our small town, there was a niche waiting to be filled: a movie rental store. This idea blossomed at a time when Netflix and online streaming had yet to fully take over, making physical movie rentals a popular choice for entertainment. So, we opened a movie rental business and called it Movie Time, LLC! Now, I was not only juggling a full-time job, I was back to volunteering as a firefighter/EMS and taking my first steps into the music industry. And now we had this movie store to run, which Beth ran during the day.

I threw my enthusiasm into everything I did, working day and night. And I had an artist for whom I was seeking gigs. None of this was easy, but I was determined to make it all work. I pushed forward, no matter the obstacles. I was confident I could make my dreams a reality, but I had one problem: the artist and his band were resistant to performing in bars. My standpoint was clear: "If you want to succeed in this industry, you've got to play in bars!" He and his band did, a few times, but they were filled with regret for having done so.

Why? Because this artist and everyone in his band were "Christians." They were heavy into their beliefs! I would use music terms to drive the focus of the band to why bars are important to play in to be able to get to the top! I managed to book the band into some pretty questionable places! I even recall a time when one of the bar owners wrote us a bounced check; that raised a lot of red flags. Ultimately, the incident became a turning point for my first artist.

Sensing I was about to lose this one, I swiftly started searching for more artists and more bars where I could build stronger connections and establish myself. Throughout this period, I worked on building relationships with the bar owners. I discovered they wanted bigger artists for their bars but didn't quite know how to bring them in. However, there were many bars that shut their doors on me, and being seen as a "nobody" representing a company no one had ever heard of made for challenging times. The artist ended up quitting me, and I focused on finding other artists. This led to building relationships with bar owners, which led to more national entertainment buying for those bars. All while managing about three or four different artists, and at this time, I had four nightclubs. This was a turning point for me.

There I was, trying to work a full-time job, run a movie store, and manage a booking/management company. Something had to go! The movie store just wasn't going anywhere, and then another movie store opened up in our town of only 1,500 residents. I knew it was time to sell! We tried everything to keep our doors open. We even made a deal with our landlord to help us purchase a truckload of clothing returns. That gave us movies and clothing to put on offer. For a short season, it was great, but no matter what we tried, we were still in a dismal place financially.

As we juggled the financial responsibilities of our growing family, our inclination towards partying, and the demands of entrepreneurship, we found ourselves in uncharted territory. Budgeting became a critical skill to master. We learned through trial and error, but with determination and perseverance, we moved toward a sustainable equilibrium. We knew something had to give. It was a sobering moment, acknowledging our dreams and desires needed to align more closely with the practicalities of our lives. We knew sacrifices would have to be made for the greater good of our family's stability and well-being.

Here's the funny part: Beth and I had plans to sell, but we hadn't made a public announcement. Then, one day, a lady entered our store. She looked up at me and asked, "How much for the clothes?" I asked, "Which ones are you interested in?" She responded, "All of your clothing!" Surprised, I asked her to give me a few minutes to calculate the cost of buying all our clothes. While doing this, somewhat jokingly, I asked if she would be interested in buying me out completely—videos, business name, and all. To my surprise, she looked at me and said, "Tell me the number!" After a series of conversations that night, she agreed to an amount, paid about 25% upfront in cash, and returned the next day—with a horse trailer—to settle the remaining amount, completely buying us out and hauling everything away!

That day, I arrived home ahead of schedule, carrying a substantial amount of cash, and casually tossed it onto the counter in front of Beth. She was surprised at me being home early and concerned about who was managing the store; she completely overlooked the pile of money I had just placed before her. It finally dawned on her that I had sold the entire store, a move that not only freed us from debt but also left us with a surplus of money! Sadly, we didn't put the extra money into a savings account nor did we invest it wisely. Our actions were quite different from the usual smart choices some people make with unexpected cash. With the casinos just a few hours away, we gathered some friends and took off on a road trip to try our luck in the thrilling world of gambling. Skipping over the specifics, we visited five or seven casinos over a couple of weekends. Fast forwarding to the aftermath, we returned home with nothing but memories of a spending spree, a nasty hangover, and the bitter reality of being back to our usual financially-strapped lives, having gone through nearly $30,000!!

Moving ahead, I started gaining traction in managing more artists and cultivating ever more positive relationships with club owners. As a result of their growing trust in me, they eventually hired me as a contractor to bring in National Country artists to their venues. This marked a pivotal moment in my career, a significant shift in my professional trajectory. Recognizing that becoming an entertainment buyer for these club owners was a less complex and risk-free endeavor, I found it to be a more manageable role. With zero front-end risks on my part, my employment hinged solely on the profitability of the shows for the clubs. As long as the venues were making money, my position remained secure.

Despite the challenges of juggling both artist management and entertainment buying, the experience proved to be a mix of difficulties and rewards. I successfully secured mini-tours for some artists alongside major national acts. One notable achievement was landing a key role for an artist as the main afterparty act for the Professional Bull Riders (PBR) event and even securing featured spots with two NFL teams—the Kansas City Chiefs and the St. Louis Rams (now formally known as the LA Rams) as National Anthem Performers for different games. Certainly, my career and reputation in the country music industry were experiencing rapid growth. Now, I found myself making a pivotal decision—I chose to leave a secure job, as a magazine delivery driver with benefits, to fully dedicate myself to advancing my music career. It was a bold and risky move, but I was ready to take my passion to the next level on a full-time basis.

Working as an entertainment buyer for four nightclubs, I found myself consistently booking national shows approximately every two weeks. These venues included Coyote Willy's in Lincoln, Nebraska;

Lightning Creek (Banjo's) in Pittsburgh, Kansas; Guitars Rock N' Country Bar in Joplin, Missouri; and Boots & Diamonds in Tulsa, Oklahoma. The frequency of these national shows contributed to the dynamic and lively atmosphere of each establishment. In addition to managing the four mentioned nightclubs, I also cultivated a significant relationship with a fifth venue, and it turned out to be my most substantial one thus far—a 5,000-seat coliseum! This new venture added another element to my portfolio and further expanded the scope of the shows and events I could bring to audiences. This venue wanted a big show about every two to three months! Highway Promotions, LLC was making it happen, and I was booking millions of dollars of entertainment.

I had the privilege of working with several artists during these times including: Stoney LaRue, Cody Johnson, Granger Smith, Parmalee, Mark Chesnutt, Turnpike Troubadours, Luke Combs, Aaron Lewis, Craig Morgan, Scotty McCreery, Phil Vassar, Josh Abbott Band, and Easton Corbin. While my business was thriving, my personal life was spiraling into a whirlwind of excess. My drinking and partying habits reached an all-time high, mirroring the success of my ventures. Regrettably, at most concerts, I found myself caught up in the revelry alongside artists, unwittingly drinking away a significant portion of my hard-earned profits. Despite all the success, there lingered within me a persistent sense of emptiness; an emptiness seemed to chase me down at every concert or at the bottom of each bottle.

As I immersed myself, almost as if I were a character in a documentary portrayed on TV, in the backstage scenes of wild partying fueled by drugs and alcohol, I experienced the highs of feeling accepted by artists and being part of the inner circle. At the same time, I was grappling with the lows of knowing the potential dangers and consequences of my choices. Despite the uncertainties, one thing remained clear: my ascent in the industry and the connections I forged with artists, agencies, and managers became my sole focus and passion. In that world, nothing else seemed to matter.

CHAPTER

5

GOING AGAINST MY BETTER JUDGMENT!

As I hit more milestones in my career, my reputation began to precede me in the music industry. Procuring entertainment became a smoother process, shows ran more seamlessly, and my understanding of the industry continued to expand. Building relationships was key! Traveling became a routine for me, shifting between various venues and making frequent trips to Nashville for meetings and conferences. It seemed like the new normal in my evolving career. Residing in a small town where everyone knows everyone, it was inevitable that many would come to hear of my flourishing career as a concert promoter.

I kept my distance. But, one day, I found myself attending a Sunday morning service at a small church in my hometown. To this day, I can't quite explain the reasoning behind my decision to go; I don't remember what prompted me to go. I just remember being there. One Sunday morning gradually extended to include Sunday nights. And then, unexpectedly, God began to orchestrate a transformation in my life that I could never have foreseen.

I received a friendly invitation to play softball. The ball fields were conveniently within walking distance from my house. I happily accepted the invitation and joined in a game. I saw it as a fun opportunity. Upon arriving the first day, I was surprised to learn the majority of those present were people from church, but several were not. Before fully participating, I took some time to observe everyone and their behavior. Initially, I couldn't help but think, "Great, some of these people might be judgmental and attempt to recruit me or push more of their beliefs on me."

The longer I watched the game, the more comfortable it felt for me to join in. I noticed that, in a lighthearted manner, they teased each other, made jokes about funny plays, and so on. I noticed that even those playing, whom I knew were not Christians, seemed to enjoy the game and the company of these church people. It struck me that I could engage in this banter and sarcasm with them. Encouraged by the friendly atmosphere, I jumped in and started playing. Before I knew it, this became a normal every-Sunday-night routine. As I became friends with everyone, regardless of their religious affiliation or lack thereof, it became evident these people were not as imposing as I had initially assumed. Surprisingly, not a single person attempted to impose their beliefs on me, and I never felt judged for the lifestyle I was leading at that time.

Nevertheless, I continued to hold on to the belief that individuals who were part of the church community or identified as Christians wouldn't accept or embrace someone with my background and experiences. This misconception weighed heavily on me, creating a barrier between myself and the possibility of finding acceptance within a community that I assumed wouldn't understand or appreciate my journey. But I could see a shared camaraderie transcended any religious differences, fostering a genuine and accepting community on the softball field. These connections evolved into genuine friendships, and before I knew it, I found myself attending more and more church services with my new friends. Indeed, the same person who once harbored a disdain for church, thinking the mere act of stepping inside would invoke some kind of cosmic reaction, found himself becoming a regular attendee.

It was quite a turnaround, wasn't it? Who would have thought— me, in church! I wasn't an every day going-to-church person, but I was heading in that direction and quickly. Honestly, I was looking forward more to the Sunday night softball games than anything. Before I knew it, I started believing the "Jesus thing." Little did I know that one of the softball games would change my life in ways that would astound me. After a service, I publicly stepped up to say "yes" to Christ, mostly because it felt like the thing everyone was doing. At that point, I still wasn't grasping; I was simply following the crowd. The longer I hung around these church people, the more I would feel like a third wheel around them. I continued to indulge in partying and drinking, persisting in behaviors I knew were likely not right, succumbing to the allure of worldly pleasures. The music industry, in particular, had a magnetic pull that repeatedly drew me back in. Little did I know, God had much bigger plans in store.

Then, one of the Sunday night softball games changed everything. In the middle of this game, the opposing team's pastor joined in to play.

Remarkably, this was someone I knew well, and he happened to be the only person of faith with whom I felt at ease having a conversation, free from judgment. In some short conversations with Pastor Beau, I began to tell him about what I was doing in the music business, and he responded back with, "Hey, why not do a Christian concert here in Stockton?" I was completely caught off guard by the suggestion. Now, I found myself grappling with this new idea. Throughout the entire game and even into the late evening hours, his words lingered in my mind, playing over and over like a persistent refrain. I remember it as an internal battle in my mind with myself. I couldn't fathom how such a thing could happen in such a small town. Where could an event like this even take place? After all, this town didn't even have a stoplight. Doubt after doubt inundated my mind. This went on for a few days! Then, one morning, I ran into the local coffee shop, and there he was: Pastor Beau! Feeling the need for more clarification about his suggestion, I approached him and asked if he remembered what he'd said to me. To my surprise, he responded, "I sure do; what do you think?" I replied, "I can't seem to shake the thought of having a concert here in Stockton; it's all I've been thinking about. You do know I specialize in securing country concerts, right?" He naturally understood and responded with a question, "Tell me, how are you currently working on your country concerts?" So I gave him a short description of the process: find a venue, find an artist, put the two together, launch tickets, and hopefully make money.

As our conversation continued, I jokingly suggested, "What if we organize a Christian concert at the church?" The idea seemed to come out of left field. It felt as though I wasn't entirely in control of my words, but rather, Someone within me was prompting and inquiring about this possibility. I was surprised by the suggestion, yet I gently reminded myself that, having lived in this town for much of my life, I knew there wasn't a suitable venue for hosting such an event. I'll never forget the expression on Pastor Beau's face. He was radiant with excitement, almost like a child on Christmas morning gazing at the biggest gift under the tree. As we were in conversation, I found myself reflecting on the confusion within me. I reminded him, "I specialize in country music concerts, you know, secular stuff!" He responded with a grin of agreement on his face, saying, "Oh, absolutely." Moreover, in that conversation, I recall countering the very idea I was suggesting. I would say things like, "I don't have the funds," or "I don't know any Christian artists." He returned with, "Well, what if I can help you? What if I had a venue to host the concert?" Truth be told, upon hearing that he could help and would help, a loud burst of sarcastic laughter escaped my mouth, accompanied by a few choice words that I won't write here, essentially conveying a firm "HECK NO, this is really going to happen!!" I was shocked that this pastor, Beau, was willing to help a guy like me—a mess, with my rough history—to put on a Christian concert in his church. Are you freaking kidding me??!!!

I just began to think how the church building wasn't going to work out as it wasn't a suitable venue, and there'd be significant obstacles to overcome. I even remember raising concerns about power needs during the conversation. At one point, I mentioned that we might need to put a hole in the wall just to run power outside for either a generator or access to clean power. Pastor Beau calmly and unequivocally fired back with words I didn't see coming. With an abundance of confidence, he boldly said, "Let's do it!"

Quickly trying to counter, considering the apparent resolution of the venue issue, my mind raced to find another obstacle. The only thing I could muster was, "I don't know any Christian artists!" It became my default defense in the face of the pastor's unexpected proposition. To my surprise, he responded, "I know some Christian artists that would be great to look into." I couldn't help but think, "Of course you do," as I realized that what started as a humorous suggestion in my mind was now turning into a real idea. The conversation concluded with him saying his offer was on the table. He assured me he would help cover costs associated with the venue, marketing, volunteers, and anything else he thought I might need. It was a generous offer, presented with a genuine willingness to support the endeavor. I then started to realize this was actually going to happen! I found myself on the verge of agreeing to organize not just any concert but one in my own hometown, and to add another layer, a Christian concert, taking place in a church! What in the world was I doing now? I distinctly recall saying to Pastor Beau, "Look, if I'm going to do this, I'm treating it like a joke because I don't really want to do it, and I can't see it happening." With a straight-faced look, he responded, "I'll take it!" Wait, had I just agreed to organize a Christian concert at a CHURCH?!?

Fast forward, I took the top ten list of Christian artists that Pastor Beau suggested and started researching. It felt like I was transported back to the earlier years of my music industry journey, a period that was then almost eight to nine years earlier. Entering this new Christian world, I found myself without connections and lacked sufficient information regarding the costs associated with artists versus potential ticket sales. It was a realm where I had no prior experience to draw upon for comparison. As I delved deeper into making connections, I found that quite a few of my existing contacts in the secular realm also had ties to the Christian side of the industry. An example: my club contact and my go-to person for all production/audio needs turned out to be a devoted Christian. When I pitched this wild idea to him, not only was he entirely on board, but he expressed a desire to cover 50% of the show's cost as well! Who does that?

With production and a substantial portion of the show costs already covered, I turned my attention to the list of the top ten artists Pastor Beau had recommended. On that list, the third artist was a heavy metal Christian band called Seventh Day Slumber. And, guess what, after calling to inquire about their cost and availability, not only were they the cheapest artist I had ever booked in my music career, but they had that date I inquired about completely open; they were ready to come and rock it out. So, putting aside my initial reservations, the show got booked for Saturday, July 10, 2016. A date that will never be forgotten and will always be a date for the books!

6

A VOICE I THINK I'D HEARD BEFORE

The day arrived, and I found myself feeling quite uncomfortable, nervous, and anxious all at once. It wasn't just any ordinary day; it involved a Christian show, and it was taking place at a church. All the elements of putting together a show were there, but the fact it was taking place in a church was more than uncomfortable for me. I remember experiencing a whirlwind of emotions as the event unfolded. Fear and joy seemed to swirl together in a mixture of great intensity. It felt as if I was looking toward my very first show.

As the day unfolded, it became clear the show would turn out to be one of the easiest events in terms of the setup on the day. The band exhibited a surprising level of kindness, a quality I hadn't encountered all that often in the secular music scene. There were no special requests for green M&M's or expensive water. Being in a small town, it would have been challenging to fulfill such requests anyway. As it came time to open the doors, a powerful nervousness crept over me. Despite my best efforts, I couldn't quite pinpoint the source of this unease.

The show kicked off, and I didn't know what to expect with the transition from country music to heavy metal; the experience was intense. It felt like my face was melting throughout the entire show; I was overwhelmed by the energy and power of the performance. Still grappling with odd feelings, I stepped outside and joined my wife in the far back parking lot during the show; this was routine for me at most shows. Due to the overwhelming intensity of my emotions, emotions I couldn't quite understand, I probably smoked a full pack of cigarettes that day. I remember struggling with the temptation to dash to a nearby store for a six-pack, but I knew I had to keep a clear mind in my home-town. I didn't want to embarrass myself or upset the church or Pastor Beau. So, I settled for stepping outside and lighting up another cigarette, trying to navigate the turmoil inside me. I can remember hearing the bass bumps from the subs inside the church. This building was rocking, and I'm sure the neighbors could hear it!

Then it happened! While outside, chatting with my wife and smoking, with my back turned to the building, the music abruptly stopped.

Silence enveloped the venue. What happened? Why did the music stop? I began to speculate: a power outage, perhaps they overloaded the system, and something blew. That feeling I'd had all day just ramped up, and I was thinking, this is it! As I was processing, I heard an audible voice saying, "John, come inside!" I asked my wife, "Did you hear who just hollered for me?" She looked over my shoulder toward the building and replied, "No one hollered for you." I quickly threw down my cigarette and raced inside. To my surprise, everything seemed normal. People were still inside, and the band was still on stage. In fact, the lead singer was sharing a story. Puzzled, I looked around, and everything appeared to be functioning properly. The music was still playing softly in the background as the lead singer, Joseph, was sharing. Standing in the back, I tried to calm down from a sudden surge of anxiety.

I tuned in to Joseph's story, which centered around a man struggling with drug and alcohol addiction. As I listened, anger welled up inside me. I felt upset that this guy, who didn't know me, was telling everyone in my hometown and my new friends about my personal struggles. Then, I noticed as his conversation carried on, that, wait, he wasn't talking about me; he was talking about himself! Now, this guy suddenly got my full attention! He went as far as saying his life got to the point where he tried to commit suicide.

Wait, let's back up here! Trying to process this guy's story, I quickly began to realize this story sounded very familiar. This was beginning to sound like me. It seemed as though the room was getting smaller as he continued talking! I started to remember myself on several occasions, thinking about suicide, even as far back as a kid stuck back in the basement. Then, it was the very next thing that pulled me back into his story when he said, "I can remember being in the back of an ambulance; after an attempt to kill myself, a man saved my life." I began to wonder who this man was, thinking it was someone in the ambulance, or firefighters, or maybe a police officer. With my history in this field, I was 100% engaged in this conversation and was excited to hear who it was who saved his life. He then posed a question to the crowd, "You wanna know

Honky Tonk Nights to Christian Lights by John A. Wilson, Jr.

45

who this man was?" And he answered, with a loud and firm voice, "His name is Jesus Christ!" HOLD THE PHONE!! WHAT?!?! I just about lost it. I was overflowing with questions, but there just wasn't enough time to process them before he continued, "How many in this room need to be set free and get to know Jesus Christ? The only man that can free you from all this!"

My heart raced so fast I thought it might burst out of my chest! I remember sweating profusely as if I had just finished running a marathon! As a matter of fact, writing this right now, I am being taken back to that very moment, and I am still tearing up. Joseph went on, "With all the stage lights, I really can't see faces, but give me a show of hands, who wants to know Jesus, who wants to ask Him into your heart?"

There it was, the moment the entire day had been building up to! I was the promoter of this show, and I wanted to raise my hand as fast as I could! I just couldn't get the strength to pull my arm up in the air! I couldn't reveal my hand. As the promoter, I couldn't afford to show any weakness. I couldn't let people see that I had these thoughts and feelings, especially not my town. As this battle was raging inside me, I noticed 23 others who did raise their hands, and when I saw this, I lost it! I was so confused. I wasn't sure how to proceed. How could an invisible guy (Jesus) help me and accept me for who I was? I was so torn between whether or not I should raise my hand and show people who I really was. I was trying to understand what I was raising my hand to! One side of me wanted to raise my hand so badly, but the other side of me had more questions.

As I was processing this, alongside me came Pastor Beau, walking from the front row of the church back to where I was standing, where I most likely looked like I'd just been hit by a bus. Pastor Beau put his arm around me and said, "Look what you did, John!" I began to weep in his arms, begged for forgiveness for my sins, and fully welcomed Jesus into my heart. That night I knew my life had been changed forever! I felt a feeling of relief no one could ever explain in words. I had so much happiness placed in me that I wasn't able to contain it! It was like a massive weight had been lifted off my shoulders, and I'd been filled with joy! I had nothing more to worry about! Was this what the other 23 kids were feeling too? This was a high that I had never felt before, and I wasn't about to let go of it!

Right now, I want you, the reader, to stop and embrace the chance to feel the same feeling I felt on July 10, 2016. I know you will have questions, as I did. But I want you to really do a self-evaluation of your heart. Are there things you have been battling? This could be any-thing—drugs, alcohol, pornography, whatever...you fill in the blank. This is just between you and Jesus. This is not the time to put this book down. Listen to me. Jesus can and will help you. Jesus will accept you as you are! Will you say yes to Jesus? Just read this out loud:

"Lord, I confess, I am a sinner. I have done so much wrong. I want to turn away from the wrong, from the wrongs I have done. I trust you can make everything right. Please come into my heart and forgive my wrong-doings. I accept you as my Lord and Savior, in Jesus' name, AMEN!"

Do you have that feeling? If you do, then you know what I was feel-ing! You are a new person in Christ. Now, before we continue with my story, I want you to know that I love you and am grateful for the oppor-tunity to welcome you to the Kingdom of Heaven. I can't wait to meet you! I want you to get plugged into a church. Find someone you know is a Christian and tell them what just happened. Don't waste time. Do this! This book will be here when you get back! GO! Tell someone so that they can celebrate with you!

"Lord, I pray for this person who has wholeheartedly asked you into their heart. Lord, I ask that you help them get connected and plugged in and that you will surround them with people who will love them, no matter what they have done. Show them your grace and power, Lord, in Jesus' name, AMEN!"

7

THE
DREAM

Welcome back! I trust you've been experiencing the Lord's work in your life. It's my hope that you're now connecting with a local church community and surrounding yourself with fellow believers who share your faith.

Let's pick up where we left off, just after the transformative event that completely changed my life. That night was a celebratory occasion for many, but I still had to process through what had happened. I still had responsibilities in finishing up the concert. It was a while before I made it home and was able to collapse into my bed. I was in a whirlwind of emotions and overwhelming questions, all compounded by exhaustion from working the show; I eventually drifted off to sleep and a dream came to me that really explained it all!

In my dream, I found myself standing in the middle of a vast, empty hay field. Suddenly, in the blink of an eye, the field transformed into a bustling scene filled with thousands upon thousands of people. I also saw food trucks at the boundaries of the field. I looked around and realized I was standing on a massive stage, gazing out at the crowd.

To the right of the stage, I saw something extraordinary—a towering 40-foot cross illuminated brightly, positioned directly in front of a large white tent and what appeared to be a swimming pool, where a line of people eagerly awaited their turn to be baptized. It was a surreal sight, and I couldn't shake the feeling that this dream held significance.

When I woke from the dream, I felt compelled to pray and reflect on its meaning. Perhaps it was a message, a vision of a country music festival intertwined with a deeper spiritual experience. This dream stirred something within me, prompting me to consider its implications and the possibilities it presented.

As I prayed and thought things over, suddenly, I heard a voice saying, "I've chosen you. Take Church Outside the Walls!" Wait, WHAT?!?!, It was surprising and a bit confusing at first. But the message struck a chord deep within me. "Take Church Outside the Walls!" Those words stayed with me, urging me to think differently about this dream and my passion for music. It was like a call to break free from the usual routines of what I used to hate with church and even Christians, to embrace a more open and inclusive way of connecting spiritually. In that moment, I felt a strong sense of purpose and duty. It was a call to step out of my comfort zone to promote a Christian Music Festival. Reaching people that were just like me, those who wouldn't set foot in a church, but would go to a music festival or concert.

With this clear direction in mind, I felt ready to embrace the challenge and to explore what it truly means to take church beyond the walls, into the wider world. I came to understand that I was meant to use the talent God had given me as a promoter for His higher purpose. It dawned on me that my ability to promote music was a gift from God, but it wasn't until I fully surrendered to His will that this gift became truly blessed and anointed. I realized that I was called to be a Christian promoter, using my skills and passion to spread the message of faith through music and events. My long-time passion for doing a music festival was finally going to happen. I can remember that exact feeling. It was like I was about to do the largest music festival the next day!

Feeling overwhelmed by the weight of this calling, I knew I needed guidance. Without delay, I reached out to Pastor Beau and shared with him the details of my dream and the unmistakable voice I had heard. Through a series of conversations and divine orchestrations, I eventually found myself connected with a couple residing all the way up in Sioux Falls, South Dakota. The link came through a lady in the church who heard about my dream. She ran a coffee vendor truck and told me I needed to connect with Alan & Vicky Greene, who—at the time I made the connection—were running the country's largest free Christian music festival, called Lifelight.

Following a number of in-person discussions and phone calls, Alan graciously took me under his wing, offering his expertise and support to help me kickstart my first festival. This partnership marked the beginning of an exciting journey and a testament to the power of God's guiding hand in bringing people together for His purpose.

In January 2017, with a vision for illuminating the community of Stockton with faith, hope and unity, I started the process of creating a nonprofit organization, called "Light the Lake." The name was inspired by the fact that our small town boasted one of the largest lakes in the southwest area of Missouri. By July 2017, our vision became a reality as we launched our very first Christian music festival in our small town. The event drew nearly 10,000 people over the course of the weekend. It was a testament to the power of faith, community, and a determination to spread God's message of love and hope. It was surreal to see everything come together just as I had dreamed a year earlier. The massive 40-foot cross stood proudly in front of the large white tent, and to our amazement, hundreds of individuals made the life-changing decision to accept Christ and be baptized right there on the spot. It was a powerful and moving sight, a testament to the impact of God's presence at the festival.

Coordinating the logistics with the small-town city officials was no small feat, especially given the influx of people pouring in from all over. Yet, through perseverance and faith, we managed to overcome every challenge to create an event that not only brought our small community together but also touched the lives of the individuals who'd come from far and wide. Faced with the challenge of managing the growing crowd, we made the decision to expand the festival the following year into a multi-day event in hopes of alleviating some of the pressure on both the attendees and the city officials. But our expectations were exceeded again. In 2018, the festival saw an astonishing turnout of nearly 23,000 people, far surpassing our projections.

The overwhelming response was a testament to the impact and significance of the festival, drawing even more individuals seeking spiritual connection and community. While the increased attendance presented new logistical challenges, it also underscored the importance of our mission to spread God's love and message to an ever-expanding audience. As the festival continued to grow in the ensuing years beyond our expectations, it became evident we needed to relocate to accommodate the increasing number of attendees. Through a period of prayer and fasting, I felt a strong calling to take the festival to the closest metro city to me— Springfield, Missouri.

Though I didn't know anyone in Springfield beyond a few radio DJs and potential partners, I trusted in God's guidance and the support of those around me. With faith as my compass, I embarked on this new chapter, believing that God would open doors and provide the connections needed to make the festival a success in its new location. I vividly recall my apprehension as I attended my first meeting with our radio partners wherein I explained the decision to relocate the festival from Stockton to the Springfield area. It was a nerve-wracking meeting for me, knowing that such a significant change could potentially strain our partnerships.

The power of that meeting lay in the fact that despite my concerns, I was met with understanding and support from our radio partners. Instead of resistance to change, there was an openness to embrace this new direction and a willingness to adapt alongside us. It was a humbling reminder of the strength of collaboration and the importance of trusting in God's guidance, even in the face of uncertainty. As a matter of fact, the radio station partners said they'd heard from the Lord as well regarding the festival needing to be relocated to this new area.

As we transitioned our ministry to Springfield, we faced some major choices. We had to figure out where and when to offer this festival, and how to make it happen with little to no connections in the area. The ministry's former name no longer fit, so we needed a new one and landed on "Light the Way Ministry." While it may not have been a name with a specific direction, it felt open-ended, allowing room for new dreams and visions. It became clear to me that Springfield wouldn't be the only festival location for this ministry. This new name reflected our broader vision of spreading light and hope to more and more communities.

8

IT WAS THE FIELD!!

Through a series of fortunate connections and meetings with key leaders in the Springfield Metro Region, I was able to secure a new location for our 2019 festival. Despite encountering a great number of challenges along the way, including some significant setbacks, we ultimately received confirmation. As I stood there, looking at the field that had appeared in my dream, I felt a profound sense of awe and gratitude. Located just seven miles outside of Springfield, in the town of Rogersville, Missouri, this field would become the new home for our festival for the next few years, marking the beginning of an exciting new chapter for Light the Way Ministry.

As we transitioned to our new location, embraced our new name, and expanded our festival to become the largest in Missouri, we also encountered significant financial challenges. The scale of the event brought with it a hefty monetary burden, unlike anything I had experienced before. In the first two years of the festival, I needed to raise only $50,000-$75,000. The new, larger event needed $350,000! God provided and the festival was held. Hard to believe, we'd gone from an attendance of maybe 200 people in a small town church to a crowd of nearly 43,000 in a significantly larger venue.

Now, this wasn't easy. Taking the last two years' festival out of my hometown, where it all began, and moving it to a metropolitan area didn't sit well with the relationships I had established with partners in Stockton. It felt like a betrayal to some, as the festival had become a cherished part of our community. However, it seemed that God wanted to grow the ministry, and the only way to do that was to relocate. The decision was fraught with challenges and emotional turmoil, but the vision for expansion and reaching a broader audience necessitated the move. Despite the difficulties, I was convinced that this was the path we were meant to take to fulfill a greater purpose.

This festival had always been offered free of charge since its inception, funded entirely by community members, partners, and sponsors. This approach was a stark contrast to my secular days in the industry, where profit and commercial success were the primary goals. Navigating this new landscape of community-driven support and sponsorship was an unfamiliar challenge for me. It required a different mindset, one focused on collaboration, generosity, and shared purpose, rather than the individualistic and profit-centric strategies to which I was accustomed. Despite the learning curve, the collective effort and spirit of giving behind the festival were inspiring and reinforced the importance of the ministry's mission.

I had to learn about both giving and receiving. Giving was particularly challenging because, despite my newfound faith, my wife (who wasn't yet a full believer but noticed changes in me) and I firmly agreed on one thing: we were not willing to give our hard-earned money to the church. This resistance stemmed from our past experiences and the high value we placed on financial security. It was a significant hurdle for us to overcome as we struggled to reconcile our beliefs with our reluctance to part with our money. However, as we became more involved in the festival and witnessed the impact of collective generosity, our perspective began to shift. Seeing how the contributions of others helped bring the festival to life and foster a sense of community helped us understand the power of giving.

It wasn't just about the money; it was about supporting something bigger than ourselves and contributing to a cause that brought people together and made a positive difference. This experience gradually opened our hearts to the idea of giving, transforming our understanding of what it means to support and be supported by a community. The fuller understanding of this didn't hit me until I was driving back from a meeting with a potential partner during the planning year of our second festival. We were short about $50,000, and the festival date was quickly approaching. My funds were running low, and the pressure was mounting. In a moment of frustration and desperation, I remember having a conversation with God—maybe it was more like yelling at God. I pleaded, "When are you going to release the funds to do what you told me to do?

Honky Tonk Nights to Christian Lights by John A. Wilson, Jr.

55

In that moment, it felt as if I was metaphorically T-boned by His voice. I heard Him clearly say, "I will release My money when you release yours!" It was a profound and humbling revelation. I realized that I had been holding onto my resources tightly, out of fear and a desire for control, even as I asked for divine provision. God was challenging me to let go, to trust Him fully, and to step out in faith by giving what I had.

I knew my next step. At that time, we had only $100 in our personal checking account, and I had to go home and tell Beth that I felt the Lord spoke to me. I needed to write a check to the church on Sunday, the church I was attending. This was a daunting conversation to anticipate, given our limited funds and Beth's skepticism about giving money to the church. Nonetheless, I felt a profound conviction that this was what God was asking of me, a step of faith that would demonstrate my trust in His provision. With a mixture of apprehension and resolve, I prepared myself to share this revelation with Beth and to act on what I believed was divine prompting.

That Sunday arrived, and as the offering time approached, I felt a wave of anxiety wash over me. Earlier that morning, I had tried to come up with reasons why I shouldn't write this check for the last $100 we had in the bank. As the offering plate made its way closer to me, I frantically looked through the check registry, hoping to find an uncleared check that would give me an excuse to hold onto our remaining funds.

The seconds ticked by, and with each passing moment, the tension grew. Finally, with a heavy heart and a mixture of reluctance and faith, I wrote the check. My hand trembled as I signed my name, fully aware of the weight of this act of obedience. As I dropped the check into the offering plate, I felt a strange mix of fear and peace. It was a moment of surrender, a step into the unknown, trusting that God would honor this leap of faith and provide for our needs in ways I couldn't yet see. This moment marked a significant turning point in my understanding of giving and receiving. It taught me that true generosity requires trust and that by releasing my grip on my own finances, I could open the door to the blessings and support God had in store for us. Because what happened the next day was nothing short of a miracle.

My phone rang, and it was from a local bank. They were calling to inquire about our festival and wanted to know about sponsorship opportunities. By the end of the call, I had secured a commitment of $5,000 from them. Shortly after, my phone rang again. This time, it was another potential sponsor, a Christian-based college, inquiring about sponsorship. They wanted to contribute and ended up giving $10,000. Next, a Christian attorney called with the same inquiries and ultimately donated over $5,000.

By the end of the week, the festival was fully funded. It was nothing short of miraculous, seeing how quickly and abundantly the needed funds came through. Each call felt like a divine confirmation that we were on the right path, and my act of faith had unlocked the provision we desperately needed. The overwhelming support from these sponsors reaffirmed that when you step out in faith, even in the face of uncertainty, God provides in ways beyond your imagination.

From that moment on, not only did I become a believer in giving to the church or ministries, but my wife, who was not yet a believer, also experienced a transformation. Witnessing the tangible provision and blessings that followed our act of faith opened her heart to the power of generosity. It was a profound turning point for both of us, solidifying our trust in God's faithfulness and His provision.

In the years that followed, giving became an integral part of our lives. It's not just about financial support; it's a reflection of our gratitude and trust in God's abundant provision. We have seen time and time again how God multiplies our offerings and blesses us beyond measure when we give with open hearts and faith-filled obedience. It's a testament to His goodness and grace, and we are grateful for the privilege of participating in His kingdom work through our giving.

There we were, in 2019, facing a significant challenge with the financial burden of the festival, which was now costing upwards of $350,000.

It was undoubtedly the biggest undertaking I'd ever faced. Somehow, against the odds, the festival came together. Fortunately, I had a line of credit from a credit card that I was able to utilize for many of the festival's logistical costs, such as equipment rentals. Using the line of credit from my credit card allowed me to ensure that I could write checks for the artists' payments that would clear without issue. In the music industry, one cardinal rule is never to write an artist a bad check. Doing so could quickly lead to being "blackballed," a term used to describe being ostracized or excluded from future opportunities within the industry. Therefore, maintaining financial integrity and honoring payments to artists was crucial to preserving my reputation and credibility in the business.

As I finished cleaning up the temporary festival office on the festival grounds, a heaviness weighed on me. Saying my goodbyes to God, to the ministry, and to the festival felt like admitting defeat. With no money left in the bank and almost $32,000 in credit card debt looming over me, I couldn't shake the feeling of failure. The decision to move the festival from Stockton to a big open field in Rogersville (a community outside Springfield) now seemed like a costly mistake.

The voices of those who had cautioned against the move from the beginning echoed in my mind, growing louder with each passing moment. Ignoring their warnings had led me to this point of financial strain and uncertainty. It was a humbling and disheartening realization, one that left me questioning my ability to continue on this mission any longer. In the quiet of the temporary festival office, there was a radio playing soft worship music in the background. The radio was tuned into a station of our actual radio partners, The Wind Radio. And it was as if the Lord himself intervened, amplifying the volume of the song that was playing, a song I recognized instantly: "God's Not Done with You Yet" by Tauren Wells. I knew then I wasn't done! I must continue on.

9

GETTING OUT OF THE WAY

Honky Tonk Nights to Christian Lights by John A. Wilson, Jr.

59

Rumors had been circulating around town about a new infectious disease that was spreading rapidly across the country. You might recall it—COVID? At first, I didn't pay much attention to the rumors, but as discussions about shutdowns began to escalate, I couldn't ignore them any longer. I was deep into planning our festival for 2020, with all the artists and production arrangements locked in. My mind was fully immersed in festival mode, focused on making it a success despite the growing concerns about COVID. I found myself faced with the daunting task of navigating around the challenges posed by the COVID pandemic while striving to host an event that could not only cover its own costs but also hopefully alleviate the debt carried over from the prior year.

Fears were piling up of the high probability of needing to cancel this festival. The effect of what that could bring felt very scary. Not only would I have the effect of canceling a show, which, in my career to date, had never happened. But how was I going to stay open with this carried-over debt? In the music industry, when you cancel shows, it's common practice to be obligated to pay the contracted amount to the artists. Now, I was confronted with the daunting prospect of potentially having to bear the financial burden of canceling a significant number of artists' contracts, productions, and all things "festival." Not to mention what this could look like for my career and reputation in the industry.

Then it happened—I received a call from the local health department instructing me to cancel the festival. It was a devastating blow. Just the previous year, the festival had drawn in nearly 43,000 people, and we were anticipating an even larger crowd for 2020. But now, all that momentum came to a screeching halt, taking me back to the feeling of doubt, I began to start to struggle to trust in God in the middle of overwhelming circumstances. With a mountain of debt looming over me and no other job to fall back on, I was consumed by some of the worst emotions I had ever experienced. I had no way out!

Then, unexpectedly, I received a phone call from a friend named Chuck. Chuck had become a significant presence in my life through our participation in several prayer meetings together. I soon learned that he was an intercessor for the 417 region, someone deeply committed to seeking God's intervention through prayer. He began to tell me about an artist who wanted to come to town for a Tent Revival. My first thought was, "What is a Tent Revival?" He began to share the vision for this event, but I quickly had to remind Chuck and myself that we were in the midst of COVID and things everywhere were shutting down. He fired back with so much passion in his voice, stating, "John, you are the guy we need for this to happen. Are you in?" I said, "Sure, but I have my doubts."

The overall focus of this event centered around the concept of "Let Us Worship," and it was clear that the government wasn't going to shut us down. Despite this assurance, only a few years into my walk with the Lord, I couldn't help but feel hesitant about the possibility of pulling off such an ambitious event. However, I reasoned with myself—what did I have to lose?

Adding to my doubts were two key factors: First, the request for my service to help bring this event to life came with a tight deadline of just two to three weeks from the time I received Chuck's call. Second, the artist involved was relatively unknown, at least within my circle in the industry. These factors only served to compound my uncertainty about the feasibility of making this event a reality. Chuck connected me to the artist, Sean Feucht, and his team. I was struck by the genuine excitement and unwavering faith exuded by his team. Talking with them reignited the same sense of excitement and faith that I had experienced at the beginning of my faith journey. It was a reminder of the power of belief and the potential for God to work in remarkable ways, even in the midst of uncertainty.

In spite of my doubts, I agreed to help; as we say in the biz, "the show must go on." We were able to navigate around a lot of the red tape associated with hosting such an event. By securing private property that was willing to host our "Tent Revival," we circumvented many of the COVID-related regulations imposed by the government. This allowed us the freedom to proceed with our plans without being hindered by bureaucratic restrictions. As the knowledge of this event started gaining traction and the preparations began to unfold, I found my doubts were gradually diminishing with each passing day. The growing excitement and momentum surrounding the event instilled a renewed sense of confidence in me. It became increasingly evident that God was at work, orchestrating the details and paving the way for something remarkable. The tent was up, the stage was set, and nearly 2,500 people started pouring under this tent.

I was in shock! This tent revival was happening, and it was something I was not expecting. This wasn't a concert, this wasn't a festival, this was ministry. I was witnessing something I had never seen before in my life, much less in my short four years of walking with Christ. As I stood in the back corner of the stage, which rose about four feet from the ground, I observed the reactions of the people as they received ministry through the music and the powerful message delivered by Sean. I witnessed people throwing representations of their addictions on the stage, everything from cigarettes, lighters, phones, and bags of weed. I remember humbling myself before the Lord, shocked at how this happened. It was a planned event I had no control over. I recalled a short conversation with God which began with me asking, "How in the world did this happen?" And the response that overwhelmed me was the voice I heard from the Lord saying: "When you get out of My way, I can move!"

10

A PROMISE MADE TO GOD

In a state of humility and shock, I couldn't help but think of this feeling of having been focused on the wrong things all this time. I took a good look at the motives I had as a promoter, and I realized the last few festivals and Christian concerts I had organized were more about building my reputation than building the kingdom and reaching souls. Now, I can't say that people weren't receiving ministry throughout this whole time. Since my salvation and surrender to our Lord and Savior up to 2024, Light the Way Ministry has had the honor of producing events where the gospel was presented to 109,575 individuals. From these events, we have been able to calculate that 3,327 decisions were made for Christ! So ministry was happening. But I began to think ministry wasn't happening for me.

Returning to the Tent Revival: after hearing that strong, resounding voice, I responded with a statement that didn't truly shake my core until most recently. I said, "Lord, I would trade 100 festivals for one of these events, just PLEASE keep my doors open." Even in the midst of such a powerful event, one that I will never forget, I was still grappling with the reality of not being able to host a festival, facing a mountain of debt, and seeing no hope of finding a way out of the darkness that seemed to weigh on me. The night came to a close, and COVID came in full swing! The world had officially SHUT DOWN! There was no church to serve, no concert to have; I wasn't sure what was next for me or Light the Way Ministry. Then there it was: a glimpse of hope started shining through, with funding options being opened up for nonprofits like mine! It was like a miracle; I came across several opportunities that wouldn't normally be available to a nonprofit like ours.

Light the Way Ministry isn't a nonprofit that addresses physical needs; our focus is on fulfilling spiritual needs, which typically means government funding isn't available to us. However, amidst the challenges posed by the pandemic, we found new opportunities opening for the live entertainment industry. We were fortunate to secure nearly $500,000 in federal funding, which helped us cover the debt from 2019 and kept our doors open throughout the difficult year of COVID-19.

Many promoters, including myself, had to get creative to stay afloat during this time, utilizing what we called "covid money." I had the privilege of teaming up with one of the largest production companies in the Christian industry, Premier Productions. Through this partnership, I was given the opportunity to host a "Drive-In Concert." These events were reminiscent of old-school drive-in movies but featured live concerts that attendees could enjoy from the comfort of their cars.

Then I received the call that Light the Way would be part of a Lauren Daigle Drive-In Concert. This event not only helped sustain our reputation but also kept us alive during a challenging period. As 2021 arrived, we were able to get back to work, and I found myself immersed in full festival planning mode once again, filled with excitement, funding available, and the feeling of being back in action.

The festival was back with a bang in 2021! It was a strong year for us, thanks to our relationships in the industry, particularly our partnership with Premier Productions. Joining forces for the 2021 festival, I knew that, with their support, I could secure the biggest names in Christian music. And indeed, we did. We locked in headliners like For King & Country and TobyMac, making it a standout year for the festival. It was a profitable year overall but, as with any festival, we still faced our share of challenges. Most importantly, I started recognizing the need for a deepening of my own spiritual growth.

I was thrilled to be back in action, and it felt like Light the Way Ministry had finally made its mark in the industry. In fact, we were now known as Missouri's Largest Christian Festival, an achievement that spoke volumes about our impact and reputation within the Christian music community. I kept focusing on growing the ministry, taking on other Christian festivals and concerts, and hiring a full team to manage the overflow of events!

As the 2023 festival unfolded, I couldn't help but be reminded of the promise I made to God back in 2020: "I would trade 100 festivals for one of these events if you just keep my doors open." A memory was sparked when I noticed an unusually long line forming on one side of our stage. If you had attended our festivals, you would have noticed two main features. First, the massive stage where the performances took place. But more importantly, you would have seen a towering 40-foot-tall illuminated cross positioned next to a swimming pool used for baptisms, all set against the backdrop of a massive white tent that we lovingly referred to as our prayer tent. These elements were central to our festival experience, serving as powerful symbols of our faith and the spiritual journey that we invited attendees to embark upon.

As I stood on the opposite side of our festival grounds, observing the line of people, my initial assumption was that they were queuing up for food from one of the vendors near the prayer tent. However, upon closer inspection, I realized they weren't waiting for food; they were lined up to receive ministry in our prayer tent. At that moment, I was struck by a powerful realization. It was then I was reminded of the promise I had made to God—I would trade 100 festivals for one of these events (referring to the tent revival in 2020). In my pursuit of recognition and success, I had lost sight of that promise. While God had faithfully kept His end of the bargain, providing opportunities and blessings beyond measure, I had faltered in keeping mine.

It was a humbling moment of reflection, a stark reminder of the importance of staying true to my commitments and aligning my priorities with God's will. Amidst the noise and distractions of the festival scene, I realized that true fulfillment and purpose could only be found in faithfully serving Him and advancing His kingdom. There I was seeing ministry happening to others, but I was starting to lose sight of it for myself. You see, I got lost in my own ways of once again trying to be heard, trying to make a name for myself, having the biggest parties. While God was faithful in keeping His promises, I was breaking mine.

In concluding the story of my transformation from feeling like a small-town nobody in a dank basement room to being the founder and leader of Light the Way Ministry, I want to emphasize the importance of staying true to one's calling and being open to God's leading. Life is filled with ups and downs, but through it all, our faith and commitment to serving God can sustain us.

While Light the Way Ministry continues to thrive today, hosting festivals and concerts, my heart is drawn toward a new vision: the revival of Tent Revivals across the country. I believe in the power of these events to remind people of their first love and to ignite a fresh passion for God. Just as I was deeply impacted by a Seventh Day Slumber concert, my journey has led me to grow in my faith, step out in obedience, and witness firsthand the power of God to set people free and bring about transformation.

I am passionate about seeing Tent Revivals spread across the nation, creating spaces where lives are changed, souls are saved, and communities are transformed by the power of God's love. It is my prayer that, through this vision, many more people will come to know the life-changing power of Jesus Christ and experience the joy of living in a relationship with Him.

CONCLUSION

Light the Way Ministry has expanded its reach since its inception, producing festivals in three states and hosting Christian concerts and tours nearly every month. As I write this story in the spring and summer of 2024, the Lord continues to guide and inspire both the ministry and my life. His direction and vision for Light the Way Ministry remain steadfast, and I am continually humbled and grateful for the opportunity to serve Him. Indeed, His hand has been evident in every step of this journey. We are continuing to expand our reach with His leading and the collaborative efforts of ministry friends, staff, and partners. Together, we remain committed to the mission of "Taking Church Outside the Walls," spreading God's love and message far beyond the confines of traditional boundaries. It's a testament to the power of unity and faith in action, and I am grateful to be part of such a transformative movement.

CEO & Founder
Light the Way Ministry
John A Wilson Jr, © 2024

Made in the USA
Columbia, SC
22 October 2024

44587088R00039